LETTERS FROM THE MASTERS OF WISDOM 1881-1888

LETTERS FROM THE MASTERS OF WISDOM 1881-1888

WITH A FOREWORD BY

ANNIE BESANT

(TRANSCRIBED AND COMPILED BY C. JINARAJADASA)

GYAN

Published by

Gyan Publishing House
5, Ansari Road
Daryaganj, New Delhi-110002
Phone: 011-47034999, 9811692060
E-mail: books@gyanbooks.com

Distribution Network
gyanbooks.com
India, USA, Canada, UK, Australia

ISBN: 978-93-6780-329-5 (HB)

First Published, 1919

2nd Impression 2024

Printed at: Gyan Press, Delhi.

LETTERS FROM THE MASTERS OF WISDOM 1881-1888
Translator: C. JINARAJADASA

LETTERS FROM
THE MASTERS OF THE WISDOM
1881—1888

LETTERS FROM
THE MASTERS OF THE WISDOM
1881—1888

WITH A FOREWORD BY

ANNIE BESANT

President of the Theosophical Society

(Transcribed and Compiled by C. Jinarājadāsa)

THEOSOPHICAL PUBLISHING HOUSE
ADYAR, MADRAS, INDIA
T.P.H., LONDON, BENARES, KROTONA, U.S.A.
INDIAN BOOK DEPOT, BOMBAY
1919

FOREWORD

I AM privileged to introduce to the world this priceless booklet of Letters from the Elder Brothers, who were the true Founders of the Theosophical Society. Many a Pilgrim on the Probationary Path will find in it much of help and inspiration, and it will serve to deepen the sense of the *reality* of our Teachers, sometimes blurred in the minds of neophytes by the tumultuous happenings in the outer world, as the notes of a vina are drowned if played in the rattle of an engine-shed. May it speak to those who have ears to hear.

ANNIE BESANT

CONTENTS

THE THEOSOPHICAL SOCIETY AND ITS WORK

LETTER I[1]

THE doctrine we promulgate being the only true one, must—supported by such evidence as we are preparing to give—become ultimately triumphant as every other truth. Yet it is absolutely necessary to inculcate it gradually, enforcing its theories—unimpeachable facts for those who know—with direct inferences deduced from and corroborated by the evidence furnished by modern exact science. That is the reason why Colonel H. S. O., who works but to revive Buddhism, may be regarded as one who labours in the true path of Theosophy far more than any other man who chooses as his goal the gratification of his own ardent aspirations for occult knowledge. Buddhism, stripped of its superstitions, is eternal truth, and he who strives for the latter is striving for Theos-Sophia, Divine Wisdom,

[1] See "Notes" at the end of the book for all numbered footnotes.

which is a synonym of Truth. For our doctrines to practically react on the so-called moral code or the ideas of truthfulness, purity, self-denial, charity, etc., we have to popularise a knowledge of Theosophy. It is not the individual determined purpose of attaining oneself Nirvana (the culmination of all knowledge and absolute wisdom)—which is after all only an exalted and glorious selfishness—but the self-sacrificing pursuit of the best means to lead on the right path our neighbour, to cause as many of our fellow-creatures as we possibly can to benefit by it, which constitutes the true Theosophist.

The intellectual portions of mankind seem to be fast drifting into two classes, the one unconsciously preparing for itself long periods of temporary annihilation or states of non-consciousness, owing to the deliberate surrender of their intellect, its imprisonment in the narrow grooves of bigotry and superstition—a process which cannot fail to [bring about] utter deformation of the intellectual principle; the other unrestrainedly indulging its animal propensities with the deliberate intention of *submitting* to annihilation pure and simple in case of failure, to millenniums of degradation after physical dissolution. Those "intellectual classes," reacting upon the ignorant masses which they attract, and which look up to them as noble and fit examples to follow, degrade and morally ruin those they ought to protect and guide. Between degrading superstition and stiil more degrading brutal materialism, the white dove of truth has hardly room where to rest her weary unwelcome foot.

It is time that Theosophy should enter the arena; the sons of Theosophists are more likely to become Theosophists than anything else. No messenger of truth, no prophet, has ever achieved during his lifetime a complete triumph—not even Buddha. The Theosophical Society was chosen as the corner-stone, the foundation of the future religions of humanity. To achieve the proposed object, a greater, wiser, and specially a more benevolent intermingling of the high and the low, of the Alpha and the Omega of Society, was determined upon. The white race must be the first to stretch out the hand of fellowship to the dark nations—to call the poor despised "nigger" brother. This prospect may not smile to all, but he is no Theosophist who objects to this principle.

In view of the ever-increasing triumph and at the same time misuse of free-thought and *liberty* (the universal reign of Satan, Eliphas Levi would have called it), how is the combative *natural* instinct of man to be restrained from inflicting hitherto unheard-of cruelty and enormities, tyranny, injustice, etc., if not through the soothing influence of a brotherhood, and of the practical application of Buddha's esoteric doctrines? For as everyone knows, total emancipation from authority of the one all-pervading power or law called God by the priests—Buddha, Divine Wisdom and enlightenment, Theosophy, by the philosophers of all ages—means also the emancipation from that of human law. Once unfettered and delivered from their dead-weight of dogmatic interpretations, personal names, anthropomorphic conceptions and salaried priests, the fundamental doctrines of all religions will be proved identical in their esoteric meaning. Osiris, Krishna, Buddha, Christ, will be shown as different names for one and the same royal highway to final bliss—NIRVANA. Mystical

Christianity, that is to say that Christianity which teaches self-redemption through our own seventh principle—this liberated Param-Atma (Augoeides) called by some Christ, by others Buddha, and equivalent to regeneration or rebirth in spirit—will be found just the same truth as the Nirvana of Buddhism. All of us have to get rid of our own Ego, the illusory apparent self, to recognise our true Self in a transcendental divine life. But if we would not be selfish, we must strive to make other people see that truth, to recognise the reality of that transcendental Self, the Buddh, the Christ or God of every preacher. This is why even exoteric Buddhism is the surest path to lead men towards the one esoteric truth.

As we find the world now, whether Christian, Mussulman, or Pagan, justice is disregarded and honour and mercy both flung to the winds. In a word, how—seeing that the main objects of the T.S. are misinterpreted by those who are most willing to serve us personally—are we to deal with the rest of humanity, with the curse known as the "struggle for life," which is the real and most prolific parent of most woes and sorrows and of all crimes? Why has that struggle become the almost universal scheme of the universe? We answer, because no religion, with the exception of Buddhism, has hitherto taught a practical contempt for the earthly life, while each of them, always with that one solitary exception, has through its hells and damnations inculcated the greatest dread of death. Therefore do we find that struggle for life raging most fiercely in Christian countries, most prevalent in Europe and America. It weakens in the Pagan lands, and is nearly unknown among Buddhists. In China during famine and where the masses are most ignorant of their own or any religion, it was remarked that those mothers who devoured their children belonged to localities where there were the most Christian missionaries to be found; where there were none, and the Bonzes alone had the field, the population died with the utmost indifference. Teach the people to see that life on this earth, even the happiest, is but a burden and delusion, that it is but our own Karma, the cause producing the effect, that is our own judge, our saviour in future lives, and the great struggle for life will soon lose its intensity. There are no penitentiaries in Buddhist lands, and crime is nearly unknown among the Buddhist Tibetans. The world in general, and Christendom especially, left for 2,000 years to the regime of a personal God, as well as its political and social systems based on that idea, has now proved a failure.

If the Theosophists say: "We have nothing to do with all this; the lower classes and inferior races (those of India, for example, in the conception of the British) cannot concern us and must manage as they can"—what becomes of our fine professions of benevolence, philanthropy, reform, etc.? Are these professions a mockery? And if a mockery, can ours be the true path? Shall we not devote ourselves to teaching a few Europeans, fed on the fat of the land—many of them loaded with the gifts of blind fortune—the rationale of bell-ringing, cup-growing, of the spiritual telephone and astral body formation, and leave the teeming millions of the ignorant, of the poor and despised, the lowly and the oppressed, to take care of themselves and their hereafter as best they know how? Never! Rather perish the T. S. with both its hapless founders than that we should permit it to become no better than an academy of magic, a hall of occultism. That we—the devoted followers of the spirit incarnate of absolute self-sacrifice, of philanthropy, divine kindness, as of all the highest virtues attainable on this earth of sorrow, the man of men, Gautama Buddha—should ever allow the T.S. to represent the *embodiment of selfishness*, the refuge of the few with no thought in them for the many, is a strange idea, my brothers. Among the few glimpses obtained by Europeans of Tibet and its mystical hierarchy of "perfect Lamas," there is one which was correctly understood and described: "the incarnations of the Bodhisattva, Padma Pani, or Avalokitesvara and of Tsong-ka-pa and that of Amitabha, relinquish at their death the attainment of Buddhahood—*i.e.*, the *summum bonum* of bliss and of individual personal felicity—that they might be born again and again for the benefit of mankind" (R.D.) *—in other words, that they might again and again

* (Rhys Davids.)

be subjected to misery, imprisonment in flesh and all the sorrows of life, provided that by such a self-sacrifice, repeated throughout long and dreary centuries, they might become the means of securing salvation and bliss in the hereafter for a handful of men chosen among but one of the many races of mankind! And it is we, the humble disciples of these perfect Lamas, who are expected to allow the T.S. to drop its noble title—that of Brotherhood of Humanity—to become a simple school of psychology. No, no, good brothers; you have been labouring under the mistake too long already. Let us understand each other. He who does not feel competent enough to grasp the noble idea sufficiently to work for it, need not undertake a task too heavy for him. But there is hardly a Theosophist in the whole Society unable to help it effectually by correcting the erroneous opinions of the outsiders, if not by actually himself propagating this idea. Oh! for the noble and unselfish man to help us effectively in India in that divine task. All our knowledge, past and present, would not be sufficient to repay him.

Having explained our views and aspirations, I have but a few words more to add. To be true, religion and philosophy must offer the solution of every problem. That the world is in such a bad condition morally is a conclusive evidence that none of its religions and philosophies—those of the *civilised* races less than any other—have ever possessed the *truth*. The right and logical explanations on the subject of the problems of the great dual principles—right and wrong, good and evil, liberty and despotism, pain and pleasure, egotism and altruism—are as impossible to them now as they were 1881 years ago. They are as far from the solution as they ever were; but there must be a consistent solution somewhere, and if our doctrines prove their competence to offer it, the world will be quick to confess that the true philosophy, the true religion, the true light, which gives truth and nothing but the truth.

LETTER II[2]

GREETINGS to the Hindu, Parsee, Buddhist, English and other Delegates and to the Fellows herewith present.

Remember that though of various nationalities and religions you are nearly all the children of one mother, India. Remember and act accordingly. You have to make of the Anniversary ceremony celebration a grand success. You have to prove to your evil wishers and enemies that your cause being strong and having taken its stand upon the rock of *truth*, indeed can never be impeded in its progress by any opposition, however powerful, if you be all united and act in concert. Be true, be loyal to your pledges, to your sacred duty, to your country, to your own conscience. Be tolerant to others, respect the religious views of others if you would have your own respected. Sons of India, of old Aryavarta, whether adopted or sons of her blood, remember that you are theosophists and that Theosophy or Brahma Vidya is the mother of every old religion, forsaken and repudiated though she may now be by most of her ungrateful children. Remember this, act accordingly and the rest will follow in due course.

With our sincere blessings,

K. H.

May no further Karma attach to those who have sinned last year in thought as well as in deed. Personally they are forgiven. Let a new year and new hopes begin for them.

K. H.

LETTER III [3]

YOU will let the " Inner Circle " know what follows by showing and leaving with them this paper. If found difficult to read my handwriting, then make a fair copy.

(I) Should means be found to go on with Esoteric Teachings last year interrupted, and should Mahatma Kut-humi find it possible to resume his correspondence, the latter can pass only through the hands of Mr. Sinnett, as hitherto. He was the chosen correspondent from the first; he resuscitated the London Lodge and worked for the Cause of the Th. Soc.; it is but just that he should reap the fruit of Karma. The Mahatma, his correspondent, could not transfer serial teaching with any degree of justice to any one else.

(II) This being settled, remains the question, What means there are to correspond even with Mr. Sinnett ? H. P. B. will not undertake the sending on and transmission of the letters ; she has shown her willingness to self-sacrifice in this direction long enough, and unless she does so of her own free-will and without reference of the question to myself, even I, her Guru for many years have no right to compel her. Damodar K. M. has the same and even more unwillingness. Since the act pertains to Karma, K. H. cannot and will not compel him, as he must not meddle with Karma. Remains . . . ; he has not reached that stage of physiological development that enables a chela to send and receive letters. His evolution has been more upon the intellectual plane, and just now a greater activity is beginning in the borderland between that and the spiritual, and his utterances will as hitherto be largely inspired by his Master. With every day he will improve. If his short-sighted friends do not spoil him by their foolish compliments and he does not yield to the seductive influences which converge towards him, there is a future for him—but he is not ready for physical transference. Moreover, when or if he once falls under the spells of the worldly life, his inspiration will cease and his name will be written on the "roll" as a failure. There is danger for him. His Master perceives it and—hesitates. There is still another person, but that person will, if even given such powers, conceal it to the last. Not every one is prepared to court and accept martyrdom which may well result in that great calamity, the interruption of one's studies and development.

(III) Whoever may be found—if one be found, to transmit to Mr. S., K. H.'s letters, neither the "Inner Circle" nor even the L. L. as a whole is in a position just now to either profit by or even calmly receive the desired instructions. A band of students of the Esot. Doctrines, who would reap any profit spiritually must be in perfect harmony and unity of thought. Each one individually and collectively has to be *utterly unselfish*, kind and full of goodwill towards each other at least—leaving humanity out of the question; there must be no party spirit among the band, no backbiting, no ill-will, or envy or jealousy, contempt or anger. What hurts one ought to hurt the other—that which rejoices A must fill with pleasure B. Is the L. L., or even its Inner Circle, in such state—which is required absolutely by our Rules and Laws? It is only owing to K. H.'s great kindness that notwithstanding the deplorable state of the L. L. was in for nearly two years and its lacking the said requisites, he still corresponded occasionally with Mr. S. The recent succession of domestic troubles would have been soon disposed of, and most of them avoided, had there been that true brotherly unity which moves a large body of men to act as one single man and as endowed with one single heart and soul. I am forced to say that only an entire change of feeling in the L. L. can bring out its potential usefulness to the great cause we have espoused. In its present state, we find it tending in the opposite direction. The L. L. is but a brilliant—most likely the *most* brilliant—orb in the Theosophical sky, but to the Parent Soc. it is an aristocratic outgrowth, an empire within an empire, which gravitating towards its own centre of fixed habits, prejudices and worldliness throws into confusion the whole Body, whereas it might so easily become the rock of salvation, the safest harbour for the thousands of its members.

It will have to change its hitherto exclusive and selfish policy if it would live. It will have to become part and parcel of the "Universal Brotherhood" if it would be a *theosophical* body. It will have to act in full harmony with the Parent Body and promote the observation of perfect solidarity and unity of thought throughout the entire Society. No gossip, no slander should be allowed, no personal predilections shown, no favouritism if it would have *us* for instructors. Mahatma Kut-humi can, of course, as an independent Adept, in his own private capacity write to whomsoever he chooses—should he find the means of doing so without infringing the good Secret Law. But he will never consent to depart from that Law even though and for the satisfaction of those who have been to him the most devoted. Let the L. L. and especially the *Inner Circle* sift the grain from the chaff, for we will have nought to do with the latter. Let them listen to friendly advice.

See what an utterly barren record it made until Mr. Sinnett's return from India—and profit by the lesson. Ye who say ye know Karma, useless to point to the various scandals at Headquarters in Bombay and Madras in palliation of your past remissness: it is no excuse.

The Managers of the P. S.[4] have made, will make, many mistakes precisely because they are alone and left without help and protection, for they might have avoided such dangerous intimacies and have none to blame but themselves that their confidence was abused. So might some of the L. L. who sinned through imprudence and enthusiasm. Human nature is exactly as weak at Adyar as in Chancery Lane or at Paris. It is truly a hard task to combine so much poor material into a strong and perfect organisation—yet the future of the Theosophic movement depends upon the members of the *Inner Circle*; if it be not organised as it ought to be, they will have to blame but themselves.

M.

———

LETTER IV [5]

To F. A.

THE day of the separation is close at hand, and I would say to you a few words. You are an officer of the L. L. and as such have a special duty and opportunity.

It is not enough that you should set the example of a pure virtuous life and a tolerant spirit; this is but negative goodness—and for chelaship will never do. You should even as a simple member—much more as an officer—learn that you may teach, acquire spiritual knowledge and strength that the weak may lean upon you, and the sorrowing victims of ignorance learn from you the cause and remedy of their pain. If you choose, you may make your home one of the most important centres of spiritualising influence in all the world. The "power" is now concentrated there, and will remain—if you do not weaken or repulse it—remain to your blessing and advantage. You will do good by encouraging the visits of your fellow members and of enquirers and by holding meetings of the more congenial for study and instruction. You should induce others in other quarters to do likewise. You should constantly advise with your associates in the Council how to make the general meetings of the Lodge interesting. New members should be taken in hand from the first by the older ones, especially selected and assigned to the duty in each case, and instructed thoroughly in what you have already learnt, so that they may be capable of participating intelligently in the proceedings of regular meetings. There is a strong disposition to slur over the ceremony of initiation in such a way as to make no serious impression upon the candidate. The method of the Parent Society may be unsuited to English prejudices, yet to fall into the opposite extreme of undignified haste is very much worse. Your ways of initiation are a standing insult to every regular Chela, and have provoked the displeasure of their Masters. It is a sacred thing with us; why should it be otherwise with you? If every Fellow took for his motto the wise words of a young boy, but one who is a fervent Theosophist, and repeated with . . . "I am a Theosophist before I am an Englishman," no foe could ever upset your Society. However, candidates should be taught, and old members always recollect, that this is a serious affair the Society is engaged in, and that they should begin the work as seriously by making their own lives Theosophical. The "Journal" is well begun, and should be continued. It should be the natural complement to that of the S. P. R., which is a bag of nuts uncracked.

Your branch should keep in correspondence with all the others in Europe; the Germania [6] can help you—the others need your help. This is a movement for all Europe—not for London only remember. The American members are under great disadvantages, and have had until now, since the Founders left, no competent leaders; your Branch can, and should help them, for they are your neighbours, and the Head Quarters have already too much to do in other quarters. A Chela will be detailed to answer general questions if the Branch deserves assistance. But remember; we are not public scribes or clerks with time to be continually writing notes and answers to individual correspondents about every trifling personal matter that they should answer for themselves. Nor shall we permit those private notes to be forwarded as freely as hitherto. Time enough to *discuss* the terms of Chelaship when the aspirant has digested what has already been given out, and mastered his most palpable vices and weaknesses. This you may show or say to all. The present is for the Branch addressed to you as its officer.

You have accepted an important service—the financial agency—and done wisely. Such aid was very needed. If the members in Europe wish well to the Mother Society, they should help to circulate its publications, and to have them translated into other languages when worthy of it. Intentions—you may tell your Fellow-Members—and kind words count for little with us. Deeds are what we want and demand. . . . . has done—poor child—more in that direction during two months than the best of your members in these five years.

The members of the London Lodge have such an opportunity as seldom comes to men. A movement calculated to benefit an English speaking world is in their custody. If they do their whole duty, the progress of materialism, the increase of dangerous self-indulgence, and the tendency towards spiritual suicide, can be checked. The theory of vicarious atonement has brought about its inevitable re-action : only the knowledge of Karma can offset it. The pendulum has swung from the extreme of blind faith towards the extreme of materialistic skepticism, and nothing can stop it save Theosophy. Is not this a thing worth working for, to save those nations from the doom their ignorance is preparing for them ?

Think you the truth has been shown to you for your sole advantage ? That we have broken the silence of centuries for the profit of a handful of dreamers only ? The converging lines of your Karma have drawn each and all of you into this Society as to a common focus that you may each help to work out the results of your interrupted beginnings in the last birth. None of you can be so blind as to suppose that this is your first dealing with Theosophy ? You surely must realise that this would be the same as to say that effects came without causes. Know then that it depends now upon each of you whether you shall henceforth struggle alone after spiritual wisdom through this and the next incarnate life, or in the company of our present associates, and greatly helped by the mutual sympathy and aspiration. Blessings to all—deserving them.

K. H.

LETTER V[7]

In view of the recent resignation of Mr. Massey and the reason for which it was given, namely, suspicion of the Mahatmas, and the inclination which has been shown by certain other members of the London Lodge to discredit the Eastern teaching and distrust its Teachers, we the undersigned members of the London Lodge, being convinced that no spiritual education is possible without absolute and sympathetic union between fellow students, desire to form an inner group.

Taking the word religion in its broadest sense and while leaving every member of the said group to follow his or her own theological system or creed—AS HERETOFORE DONE IN ALL THE THEOSOPHICAL SOCIETIES—we desire nevertheless to establish a bond of true brotherly union of such a nature as to realise those conditions, which we are convinced are unattainable in the London Lodge as it is constituted.

For this Inner Group—the Adytum of the London Lodge—we humbly crave the unchartered recognition of the Mahatmas, our Beloved Teachers: requesting them further to grant us special permission to form our own bye-laws and choose our own council; and while remaining individually subject to the rules and bye-laws of the London Lodge, the group as such to be independent of the London Lodge in its special work.

The fundamental principle of the New Group to be implicit confidence in the Mahatmas and their teachings, and unswerving obedience to their wishes in all matters connected with spiritual progress.

N.B. Should however there be a sincere conviction on the part of any member that he, or she, cannot conscientiously render this unswerving obedience in all matters of spiritual progress, such member may withdraw from the inner circle, with the assurance and knowledge that the imputation of dishonourable conduct will not be charged against him or her.

H. P. Blavatsky

—PROVIDED HE OR SHE DOES NOT MAKE ANY PART OF THE TEACHINGS PUBLIC BY WORD OR LETTER WITHOUT SPECIAL PERMISSION FROM THE UNDERSIGNED.—K. H.

Finally in submitting this prayer to our revered Masters we earnestly request them, if it meets with their approval, to confirm it with their signatures and to consent to continue their teachings as heretofore so long as there shall remain one faithful member in this group.

APPROVED. THE COVENANT IS MUTUAL. IT WILL HOLD GOOD SO LONG AS THE ACTIONS OF THE UNDERSIGNED ARE ACCORDANT WITH THE PLEDGES IMPLIED IN "THE FUNDAMENTAL PRINCIPLES OF THE GROUP," AND BY THEM ACCEPTED.—K.H.

APPROVED. M.

THE PATH OF DISCIPLESHIP

LETTER VI [8]

THE process of self-purification is not the work of a moment, nor of a few months but of years—nay extending over a series of lives. The later a man begins the living of a higher life, the longer must be his period of probation for he has to undo the effects of a long number of years spent in objects diametrically opposed to the real goal. The more strenuous one's efforts and the brighter the result of his work, the nearer he comes to the Threshold. If his aspiration is genuine—a settled conviction and not a sentimental flash of the moment—he transfers from one body to another the determination which finally leads him to the attainment of his desire. B . . . S . . . has seen me in my own physical body and he can point out the way to others. He has been working unselfishly for his Fellowmen thro' the Theosophical Society and he is having his reward tho' he may not always notice it.

K. H.

LETTER VII [9]

LAST spring—March the 3rd—you wrote a letter to me and entrusted it to "Ernest".[10] Though the paper itself never reached me —nor was it ever likely to, considering the nature of the messenger—its contents have. I did not answer it at the time, but sent you a warning through Upasika.[11]

In that message of yours it was said that since reading *Esot. Bud:* and *Isis* your "one great wish had been to place yourself *under me as a chela, that you might learn more of the truth*". "I understand from Mr. S.," you went on, "that it would be almost impossible to become a chela without going out to India." You hoped to be able to do that in a few years, though for the present ties of gratitude bind you to remain in this country, etc.

I now answer the above and your other questions.

(1) It is *not* necessary that one should be in India during the seven years of probation. A *chela* can pass them anywhere.

(2) To accept any man as a chela does not depend on my personal will. It can only

be the result of one's personal merit and exertions in that direction. *Force* any one of the "Masters" you may happen to choose; do good works in his name and for the love of mankind; be pure and resolute in the path of righteousness (as laid out in *our* rules); be honest and unselfish; forget your self but to remember the good of other people—and you will have *forced* that "Master" to accept you.

So much for candidates during the periods of the undisturbed progress of your Society. There is something more to be done, however, when Theosophy, the Cause of Truth is, as at the present moment, on its stand for life or death before the tribunal of Public opinion—that most flippantly cruel, prejudiced and unjust of all tribunals. There is also the collective karma of *the caste you belong to* [12] to be considered. It is undeniable that the cause you have at heart is now suffering owing to the dark intrigues, the base conspiracy of the Christian clergy and missionaries against the Society. They will stop before nothing to ruin the reputation of the Founders. Are you willing to atone for *their* sins? Then go to Adyar for a few months. "The ties of gratitude" will not be severed, nor even become weakened for an absence of a few months if the step be explained plausibly to your relative. He who would shorten the years of probation has to make sacrifices for Theosophy. Pushed by malevolent hands to the very edge of a precipice, the Society needs every man and woman strong in the cause of truth. It is by *doing* noble actions, and not by determining that they shall be done, that the fruits of meritorious actions are reaped. Like the "true man" of Carlyle, who is not to be seduced by ease, "difficulty, abnegation, martyrdom, death are the *allurements* that act" during the hours of trial on the heart of a true chela.

You ask me, "What rules I must observe during this time of probation, and how soon I might venture to hope that it could begin." I answer: You have the making of your own future in your own hands, as shown above, and every day you may be weaving its woof. If I were to *demand* that you should do one thing or the other, instead of simply advising, I would be responsible for every effect that might flow from the step, and you acquire but a secondary merit. Think, and you will see that this is true. So cast the lot yourself into the lap of Justice, never fearing but that its response will be absolutely true. Chelaship is an educational as well as a probationary stage, and the chela alone can determine whether it shall end in adeptship or failure. Chelas, from a mistaken idea of our system, too often watch and wait for orders, wasting precious time which should be taken up with personal effort. Our cause needs missionaries, devotees, agents, even martyrs, perhaps. But it cannot demand of any man to make himself either. So now choose and grasp your own destiny—and may our Lord's the Tathâgata's memory[13] aid you to decide for the best.

K. H.

LETTER VIII[14]

SINCE your intuition led you in the right direction and made you understand that it was *my desire* you should go to Adyar *immediately*, I may say more. The sooner you go to Adyar the better. Do not lose one day more than you can help. Sail on the 5th, if possible. Join Upasika at Alexandria. Let no one know that you are going, and may the blessing of our Lord and my poor blessing shield you from every evil in your new life.

Greeting to you, *my new chela.*

K. H.

LETTER IX [15]

SIGH not for Chelaship ; pursue not that, the dangers and hardships of which are unknown to you. Verily many are the chelas offering themselves to us, and as many have failed this year as were accepted on probation. Chelaship unveils the inner man and draws forth the dormant virtue as well as the dormant vice. Latent vice begets active sins and is often followed by insanity. Throw a glance round, make an enquiry at Bareilly and Cawnpore, and judge for yourself. Be pure, virtuous, and lead a holy life and you will be protected. But remember, he who is not as pure as a young child better leave chelaship alone. I have forbidden at Headquarters to send over any letters to me.

K. H.

P.S.[16] The process of self-purification is not the work of a moment, nor of a few months, but of years, nay extending over a series of lives. The later a man begins living the higher life the longer must be his period of probation. For he has to undo the effects of a long number of years spent in objects diametrically opposed to the real goal.

LETTER X[17]

HE who damns himself in his own estimation and agreeably to the recognised and current code of honour to save a worthy cause may some day find out that he has reached thereby his loftiest aspirations.

Selfishness and the want of self-sacrifice are the greatest impediments on the path of adeptship.

K. H.

LETTER XI [18]

My chelas must never doubt, nor suspect, nor injure our agents by foul thoughts. Our modes of action are strange and unusual, and but too often liable to create suspicion. The latter is a snare and a temptation. Happy is he whose spiritual perceptions ever whisper truth to him! Judge those directly concerned with us by that perception, not according to your worldly notions of things.

K. H.

INDIA AND THE THEOSOPHICAL MOVEMENT

LETTER XII [19]

DEGRADE not truth by forcing it upon unwilling minds. Seek not to secure help from those whose hearts are not patriotic enough to unselfishly work for the good of their country-men. "What good can we do?" is asked. "What benefit can we confer upon humanity, or even our own country?" Luke-warm patriots, verily, are they. In the presence of his country perishing in its nationality for want of vitality, and the infusion of fresh forces, the *patriot* catches at a straw. But are there *any true patriots* in Bengal? Had there been many, we would have sent you here before now; we would have hardly allowed you to remain three years in India without visiting Calcutta, the city of great intellects and—no hearts. You may read this to them.

K. H.

LETTER XIII [20]

Do not forget that all the good results that are in store for our India . . . are all due to her [H. P. B.'s] individual efforts. You can hardly show her enough respect and gratitude, or more than she is entitled to . . . You will have to carefully impress them with the sense of the exalted position she ought to—if she does not—hold among those Hindus who have remained true to the Past, care not for the Present, and work but for the Future, which will be great and glorious if she is only supported and helped by them.

K. H.

LETTER XIV [21]

EFFECTS of the cycle: Mr. Sinnett was given notice by his Proprietors to quit the Editor's office 12 months hence—*for supporting the natives* and being a theosophist. Unless a native capitalist comes out to start a rival paper —one that would crush the *Pioneer*—with

Mr. Sinnett as its editor, I will despair of India indeed. The above is *secret* entrusted to your honour. But I will write to Norendro N.S.[22] and have a talk with him upon the subject. Till then—not a word.

K. H.

LETTER XV[23]

TURN to the *Pioneer* of August 7th and read with attention the article " Indo-British India ". Think you *the Editor* would have ever written it had he been left merely to the acquaintance and *friendly* feelings of the Hindus—your and *my* countrymen ? And think you, that a series of such articles, in such a (hitherto) *conservative* paper, written by one so haughty though at the same time so noble and so just a man would do *no* good to any one ? Such is the first political fruit of the Society you have the honour to belong to. And, instead of doubting, thank heaven, if you have a patriotic heart beating in your breast, that there are a few " Brothers " yet left to India, to watch over her interests, and protect her in hours of danger ; since in their hourly increasing selfishness none of her sons seem to ever remember they have a Mother—degraded, fallen down, and trampled under the feet of all, of conquerors and of the conquered—still a MOTHER.

Take care . . . Doubt is a dangerous cancer. One begins by doubting a *peacock*, and ends by doubting—

KOOT HOOMI

LETTERS OF PERSONAL COUNSEL

LETTER XVI[24]

I COME to you not alone of my own accord and wish, but also by order of the Maha Chohan, to whose insight the future lies like an open page. At New York you demanded of M. an objective proof that his visit to you was not a maya—and he gave it;[25] unasked, I give you the present one: tho' I pass out of your sight this note will be to you the reminder of our conferences. I now go to young Mr. Brown to try his intuitiveness. To-morrow night when the camp is quiet and the worst of the emanations from your audience have passed away, I shall visit you again for a longer conversation, as you must be forewarned against certain things in the future. Fear not and doubt not as you have feared and doubted at supper last night: the first month of the coming year of your era will have hardly dawned when two more of the "enemies"[26] will have passed away. Ever be vigilant, zealous and judicious; for remember that the usefulness of the Theosophical Society largely depends upon your exertions, and that our blessings follow its suffering "Founders" and all who help on their work.

K. H.

LETTER XVII [27]

WATCH for the signal: prepare to follow the messenger who will come for you.

K. H.

LETTER XVIII [28]

BEYOND asking you to tell . . . that I have received all his letters (that of February 15th included) but have had not even a moment's time to give him, I have nothing of the nature of a "commission" for you to execute in London. That, of course, is M's province; and he has, under the orders of the Maha-Chohan, left you the widest discretion in the full knowledge that you will vindicate the policy of the Society.

If you will recall our conversation of the *second* night at Lahore, you will observe that everything has happened at London as foretold. There have always been in that quarter latent potentialities of destruction, as well as of a constructive nature, and the best interests of our movement required the bringing of all to the surface. As your charming new friends at Nice, who frequent Monte Carlo and the gambling *cercles*, would say, the players have now—*cartes sur table.*

Those who have been so perplexed and puzzled over our policy as regards the London Lodge, will understand its necessity better when they become better acquainted with the very occult art of drawing out the hidden capacities and propensities of beginners in occult study. Do not be surprised at anything you may hear from Adyar, nor discouraged. It is possible—though we try to prevent it within the limits of karma—that you may have great domestic annoyances to pass through. You have harboured a traitor and an enemy under your roof for years, and the missionary party are more than ready to avail of any help she may be induced to give. A regular conspiracy is on foot. She is maddened by the appearance of Mr. Lane Fox and the powers you have given to the Board of Control.

We have been doing some phenomena at Adyar since H. P. B. left India, to protect Upasika from the conspirators.

And now act discreetly under your instructions, depending rather upon your notes than your memory.

K. H.

LETTER XIX [29]

TO HENRY OLCOTT

AGAIN, as you approach London I have a word or two to say to you. Your impressibility is so changeful that I must not wholly depend upon it at this critical time. Of course you know that things were so brought to a focus as to necessitate the present journey, and that the inspiration to make it came to you, and to permit it, to the Councillors *from without.* Put all needed restraint upon your feelings, so that you may do the right thing in this Western imbroglio. Watch your first impressions. The mistakes you make spring from failure to do this. Let neither your personal predilections, affections, suspicions nor antipathies affect your action.

Misunderstandings have grown up between fellows both in London and Paris which imperil the interests of the movement. You will be told that the chief originator of most, if not of all these disturbances, is H. P. B. This is not so; though her presence in England has, of course, a share in them. But the largest share rests with others, whose serene unconsciousness of their own defects is very marked and much to be blamed. One of the most valuable effects of Upasika's mission is that it drives men to self-study and destroys in them blind servility for persons. Observe your own case, for example. But your revolt, good friend, against her "infallibility"—as you once thought it—has gone too far, and you have been unjust to her, for which I am sorry to say, you will have to suffer hereafter, along with others. Just now—on deck, your thoughts about her were dark and sinful, and so I find the moment a fitting one to put you on your guard.

Try to remove such misconceptions *as you will find*, by kind persuasion and an appeal to the feelings of loyalty to the Cause of truth, if not to us. Make *all* these men feel that we have no favourites, nor affections for persons, but only for their good acts and humanity as a whole. But we employ agents—the best available. Of these, for the past thirty years, the chief has been the personality known as H. P. B. to the world (but otherwise to us). Imperfect and very troublesome, no doubt, she proves to some; nevertheless, there is no likelihood of our finding a better one for years to come, and your theosophists should be made to understand it. Since 1885 I have not written, nor caused to be written save through her agency, direct or remote, a letter or line to anybody in Europe or America, nor communicated orally with, or thro' any third party. Theosophists should learn it. You will understand later the significance of this declaration, so keep it in mind. Her fidelity to our work being constant, and her sufferings having come upon her thro ' it, neither I nor either of my Brother Associates will desert or supplant her. As I once before remarked, *ingratitude* is not among our vices. With yourself our relations are direct, and have been, with the rare exceptions you know of, like the present, on the psychical plane, and so will continue thro' force of circumstances. That they are so rare—is your own fault as I told you in my last. To help you in your present perplexity: H. P. B. has next to no concern with administrative details, and should be kept clear of them, so far as her strong nature can be controlled. But this *you must tell to all:—with occult matters she has everything to do.* We have *not* abandoned her. She is *not* given over to chelas. She is *our direct agent.* I warn you against permitting your suspicions and resentment against " her many follies " to bias your intuitive loyalty to her. In the adjustment of this European business, you will have two things to consider—the external and administrative, and the internal and psychical. Keep the former under your control and that of your most prudent associates, jointly; *leave the latter to her*. You are left to devise the practical details with your usual ingenuity. Only be careful, I say, to discriminate when some emergent interference of hers in practical affairs is referred to you on appeal, between that which is merely exoteric in origin and effects, and that which beginning on the practical tends to beget consequences on the spiritual plane. As to the former you are the best judge, as to the latter, she.

I have also noted, your thoughts about the "Secret Doctrine". Be assured that what she has not *annotated* from scientific and other works, we have given or *suggested* to her. Every mistake or erroneous notion, corrected and explained by her from the works of other theosophists *was corrected by me, or under my instruction*. It is a more valuable work than its predecessor, an epitome of occult truths that will make it a source of information and instruction for the earnest student for long years to come.

P. S. . . . is in great mental distress once more, because of my long silence, not having a clear intuition developed (as how should he after the life he has lead?). He fears he is abandoned, whereas he has not been lost sight of for one moment. From day to day he is making his own record at the "Ashram" from night to night receiving instructions fitted to his spiritual capabilities. He has made occasional mistakes, *e.g.*, one recently, in helping thrust out of the Headquarters house, one who deserved a more charitable treatment, whose fault was the result of ignorance and psychical feebleness rather than of sin, and who was a strong man's victim. Report to him, when you return, the lesson taught you by △ at Bombay,[30] and tell my devoted tho' mistaken "son" that it was most theosophical to give her protection, most untheosophical and selfish to drive her away.

I wish you to assure others T.T., R.A.M., N.N.S., N.D.C., I.N.C., U.U.B., T.V.C., P.V.S., N.B.C., C.S., C.W.L., D.N.G., D.H., S.N.C., etc., among the rest, not forgetting the other true workers in Asia, that the stream of Karma is ever following on and we as well as they must win our way toward liberation. There have been sore trials in the past, others await you in the future. May the faith and courage which have supported you hitherto endure to the end.

You had better not mention for the present this letter to anyone—not even to H.P.B. unless she speaks to you of it herself. Time enough when you see occasion arise. It is merely given you, as a warning and a guide; to others, as a warning only, for you may use it discreetly if needs be.

K. H.

Prepare, however, to have the authenticity of the present denied in certain quarters.

LETTER XX [31]

I HAVE watched your many thoughts. I have watched their silent evolution and the yearnings of your inner soul; and since your pledge permits me to do so, having a few things to tell you concerning yourself and those you love—I take the opportunity, one of the last there are to write to you directly, to say a few words. You know of course that once that H. P. B.'s aura in the house is exhausted you can have no more letters from me.

I want you to be acquainted with the situation as it now stands. Your loyalty to the cause entitles you to this.

First about your friend . . . Poor child! By placing so constantly her personality over and above her inner and better Self—tho' she knows it not—she has done all she could for the last week to sever herself from us for ever. Yet so pure and genuine she is that I am ready to leave a chink in the door she slams unconsciously to herself into her own face, and await for the entire awakening of that honest nature whenever that time comes. She is without artifice or malice; entirely truthful and sincere, yet at times quite false to herself. As she says her ways are not *our* ways, nor can she comprehend them. Her personality coming in so strong in her ideas of the fitness of things, she cannot certainly understand our acts on our plane of life. Tell her in all kindness, that if H. P. B. (as an example) was wrong last night—as she always is, from the Western point of view, in her everlasting natural impulses apparently so rude and indelicate—she did it after all at her Master's direct order. She never stops one moment to consider the propriety of things when concerned in carrying out such orders. In the eyes of you, the civilised and cultured portion of mankind, it is the one unpardonable sin; in our sight—*i.e.*, uncultured Asiatics—it is the greatest virtue; for before it became with her a habit, she used to suffer in *her* Western nature and perform it as self-sacrifice of her personal reputation. But, if she was wrong . . . was not right either. She allowed her womanly pride and personality—which were entirely out of question, at any rate out of H. P. B.'s thoughts—to get mixed up and prime in a question of pure rules and discipline. . . . and . . . were more to be blamed than either of the two. You must remember that both have set themselves voluntarily apart from worldly society . . . for a specific object; and to say nothing of the relative decency or indecency of any social custom of any country, there are rules of conduct controlling chelas which cannot be departed from in the slightest degree. I pray you, to use your influence with her, if you wish her good, to have her book published before the year 1885. Tell her also, since she has cut herself away from me, that she will have in good time the help of the Adept who writes stories with H.P.B. Yet since *novellettes* interest her more than metaphysics she has no need for the present of . . . .'s help. He is certainly more wanted in London . . .

Having overheard your conversation with H. P. B. on the night of her arrival, I may say that you are right. To your aged mother, who has trodden with you in many stony paths of belief and experience since your childhood, you owe a great duty. Not a blind and unjust obedience whose consequences may be most harmful to her as to yourself; but a dutiful assiduity, and loving help to develop her spiritual intuitions and prepare her for the future. Many crosses and domestic sorrows have left their bleeding scars on her heart . . . She and you have earned happy rewards for your kindness to our messengers, and Karma will not forget them. But *look to the future*; see to it that the continual performance of duty under the guidance of a well developed Intuition shall keep the balance well poised. Ah! if your eyes were opened, you might see such a vista of potential blessings to yourselves and mankind lying in the germ of the present hour's effort, as would fire with joy and zeal your souls! Strive towards the Light, all of you brave warriors for the Truth, but do not let selfishness penetrate into your ranks; for it is selfishness alone that throws open all the doors and windows of the inner Tabernacle and leaves them unshut.

To you personally, child, struggling thro' darkness to the Light, I would say, that the Path is *never* closed; but in proportion to one's previous errors so is it harder to find and to tread. In the eyes of the "Masters" no one is ever "utterly condemned". As the lost jewel may be recovered from the very depths of the tank's mud, so can the most abandoned snatch himself from the mire of sin, if only the precious Gem of Gems, the sparkling germ of the Atma, is developed. Each of us must do *that* for himself, each *can* if he but will and persevere. Good resolutions are mind-painted pictures of good *deeds*: fancies, day-dreams, whisperings of the *Buddhi* to the *Manas*. If we encourage them they will not fade away like the dissolving mirage in the Shamo desert, but grow stronger and stronger until one's whole life becomes the expression and outward proof of the divine motive within. Your acts in the past have been the natural fruit of an unworthy religious ideal, the result of ignorant misconception. They cannot be obliterated, for they are indelibly stamped upon the record of Karma, and neither tears nor repentance can blot the page. But you have the power to more than redeem and balance them by future acts. Around you are acquaintances, friends and associates—in, and outside, the T.S. who have committed the same and even more grievous faults, thro' the same ignorance. Show them the dreadful consequences of it, point them to the Light, lead them to the Path, teach them, be a missionary of love and charity, thus in helping others win your own salvation. There are innumerable pages of your life record still to be written up, fair and blank they are as yet. Child of your race and of your age, seize the diamond pen and inscribe them with the history of noble deeds, days well-spent, years of holy striving. So will you win your way ever upward to the higher planes of spiritual consciousness. Fear not, faint not, be faithful to the ideal you can now dimly see. You have much to unlearn. The narrow prejudices of your people bind you more than you suspect. They make you intolerant, as last night, of the petty offences of others against your artificial standards of propriety, and disposed to lose sight of essentials. You are not yet able to appreciate the difference between inner purity and "outer *culture*". Were the "Masters" to judge *you* by your own social canons, where would you stand? The very Society whose hypocritical rules of propriety you stand for so vehemently, is a festering mass of brutishness within a shell of decency. From their ignorant and malevolent intolerance you appeal to us, because your intuition tells you that they will not accord you justice. Learn then to look at men below the surface, and to neither condemn nor trust on appearances. Try, child. HOPE, and accept my blessing.

K. H.

LETTER XXI [32]

I HAVE pleasure in granting, in part at least, your request. Welcome to the territory of our Kashmir Prince. In truth my native land [33] is not so far away but that I can assume the character of host. You are not now merely at the threshold of Tibet, but also of all the wisdom it contains. It rests with yourself how far you shall penetrate both, one day. May you deserve the blessings of our *Chohans*.

K. H.

LETTER XXII [34]

I HAVE told you through D. to have patience for the fulfilment of your desire. From this you ought to understand that it cannot be complied with for various reasons. First of all it would be a great injustice to Mr. S. who, after three years' devoted work for the Society, loyalty to myself and to the cause, begged for a personal interview and was refused. Then

I have left Mysore a week ago, and where I am you cannot come since I am on my journey and will cross over at end of my travels to China and thence home. On your last tour you have been given so many chances for various reasons—we do not do so much (or so little if you prefer) even for our Chelas, until they reach a certain stage of development necessitating no more use and abuse of power to communicate with them. If an Eastern, especially a Hindu, had even half a glimpse but once of what you had, he would have considered himself blessed the *whole of his life.*

Your present request *mainly rests* upon the *complaint* that *you are not able to write* with a full heart, although perfectly convinced yourself, *so as* to leave no room in the minds of *your countrymen* for doubt. Pray, can you propose any test which *will be* a thorough and perfect proof for all? Do you know what results would follow from your being permitted to see me here in the manner suggested by you and your reporting that event to the English Press? Believe me they would be disastrous for *yourself*. All the evil effects and bad feelings which this step would cause would recoil upon you and throw back your own *progress* for a considerable time and no good will ensue. If *all that you saw* was imperfect *in itself* it was due to previous causes. You saw and recognised me twice at a distance, you knew it was I and no other ; what more do you desire? If when after visiting Col. Olcott I passed over to your room and my voice and words pronounced—" Now you see me before you in flesh, look and assure yourself that it is I "—failed to *impress you*, and when the letter put into your hand awoke you at last but failed again to make you turn your face, your nervousness paralyzing you for a moment, the fault is surely yours, not mine. I had no right to act upon you phenomenally or to psychologise you. *You are not ready*, that is all. If you are earnest in your aspirations, if you have the least spark of intuition in you, if your education of a lawyer is complete enough to enable you to put facts in their proper sequence and to present your case as strongly as you in your innermost heart believe it to be, then you have material enough to appeal to any intellect capable of perceiving the continuous thread underneath the series of your facts. For the benefit of such people only you have to write, not for those who are unwilling to part with their prejudices and preconceptions for the attainment of truth from whatever source it may come. It is not our desire to convince the latter, for no fact or explanation can make a blind man see. Moreover our existence would become extremely intolerable, if not impossible, were all persons indiscriminately *convinced*. If you cannot do even this much from what you *know*, then no amount of evidence will ever enable you to do so. You can say truthfully and as a man of honour: "I have seen and recognised my Master, was approached by him and even touched." What more would you want? Anything more is impossible for the present. Young friend! Study and prepare and especially *master your nervousness*. One who becomes a slave to any physical weakness never becomes the master of even the lower powers of nature. Be patient, content with little and—*never ask for more* if you would hope to ever get it. My influence will be over you and this ought to make you calm and resolute.

K. H.

LETTER XXIII [35]

PERSEVERE and whether " on the right track " or not—if sincere you will succeed for I will help you. Your country needs help, and you are possessed of that *power* of mind which is the element of greatness and which in you ought to be shown in the stern resolution with which you can go forward to your end thro' all obstacles and overbearing all opposition. *Try* and you will succeed.

K. H.

LETTER XXIV [36]

So then, you really imagined when you were allowed to call yourself my chela—that the black memories of your past offences were either hidden from my notice or that I *knew* and still *forgave* ? Did you fancy that I connived at them ? Foolish . . . ! thrice foolish ! It was to help save you from your viler Self, to arouse in you better aspirations ; to cause the voice of your offended " soul " to be heard ; to give you the stimulus to make *some* reparation . . . for these *only* your prayer to become my chela was granted. We are the agents of Justice, not the unfeeling lictors of a cruel god. Base as you have been, vilely as you have misused your talents . . . blind as you have been to the claims of gratitude, virtue and equity, you have still in you the qualities of a good man—(*dormant* indeed, so far !)—and a useful chela. But how long your relations with us will continue—depends alone upon yourself. You may struggle up out of the mire, or glide back into depths of vice and misery now inconceivable to your imagination . . . Remember, . . . that you stand before your Atma, which is your judge, and which no smiles, nor falsehoods, nor sophistries can deceive. Hitherto you had but bits of *chits* from me and—*knew me not*; now you know me better, for it is I who accuse you before your awakened conscience. You need make no lip-promises to *It* or me, no half-way confessions. Though . . . you shed oceans of tears and grovel in the dust, this will not move a hair's breadth the balance of Justice. If you would recover the lost ground do two things: make the amplest, most complete reparation . . . and to the good of mankind devote your energies . . . Try to fill each day's measure with pure thoughts, wise words, kindly deeds. I shall neither order, nor mesmerize, nor sway you. But unseen and when you have perhaps come —like so many others—to disbelieve in my existence, I shall watch your career and sympathise in your struggles. If you come out victorious at the end of your probation I shall be the readiest to welcome you. And now—there run two paths before you, *choose!* When you have chosen you may consult your visible official superior—H. S. Olcott, and I will instruct him thro' his Guru to guide and send you on . . .

You aspire to be a missionary of theosophy; be one—if you can be one in *fact*. But rather than go about preaching with a heart and a life that belie your professions—*conjure the lightning to strike you dead*, for every word will become your future accuser. Go and consult with Col. Olcott—confess your faults before *that good man*—and seek his advice.

K. H.

LETTER XXV[37]

To H. R.

From one who will ever watch over and protect him if he goes on in the path of duty to his country and righteousness to his Brethren,

K. H.

LETTERS ABOUT D. M. K.

LETTER XXVI [38]

DAMODAR,

I want you to have this followed by Subram's statement. You may take out something else from the *Supplement*.

K. H.

LETTER XXVII [39]

DO not feel so dejected, my poor boy, no need for that. As Mr. Sinnett rightly says in his *Esoteric Buddhism*, the higher spiritual progress must be accompanied by intellectual development on a parallel line. You have now the best opportunities for doing that where you are working. For your devotion and unselfish labour, you *are* receiving help, silent tho' it be. Your time is not yet come. When it does, it shall be communicated to you. Till then make the best of the present favourable opportunity to improve yourself intellectually while developing your intuitions. Remember that no effort is ever lost and that for an occultist there is no past, present or future, but ever an Eternal Now. Blessings.

K. H.

LETTER XXVIII [40]

D. HAS undoubtedly many faults and weaknesses as others have. But he is unselfishly devoted to us and to the cause, and has rendered himself extremely useful to Upasika. His presence and assistance are indispensably necessary at the Headquarters. His inner self has no desire to domineer, though the outward acts now and then get that colouring from his excessive zeal which he indiscriminately brings to bear upon everything, whether small or great. It must, however, be remembered that, inadequate as our "instruments" may be to our full purpose, they are yet the best available, since they are but the evolution of the times. It would be most desirable to have better " mediums " for us to act through ; and it rests with the well-wishers of the Theosophical *Cause* how far they will work unselfishly to assist in her higher work and thus hasten the approach of the eventful day. Blessings to all the faithful workers at the Headquarters.

K. H.

LETTER XXIX [41]

THE poor boy has had his *fall*. Before he could stand in the presence of the " Masters " he had to undergo the severest trials that a neophyte ever passed through, to atone for the many questionable doings in which he had over-zealously taken part, bringing disgrace upon the sacred science and its adepts. The mental and physical suffering was too much for his weak frame, which has been quite prostrated, but he will recover in course of time. This ought to be a warning to you all. You have believed " not wisely but too well ".

To unlock the gates of the mystery you must not only lead a life of the strictest probity, but learn to discriminate truth from falsehood. You have talked a great deal about Karma but have hardly realised the true significance of that doctrine. The time is come when you must lay the foundation of that strict conduct —in the individual as well as in the collective body—which, ever wakeful, guards against conscious as well as unconscious deception.

K. H.

GENERAL

LETTER XXX [42]

My Dear Brother,

I have to apologize for the delay in answering several of your letters. I was greatly occupied with business entirely foreign to occult matters, and which had to be transacted in the usual dry, matter-of-fact way.

Moreover, I do not find much to answer in your letters. In the first you notify me of your intention of studying Advaita Philosophy with a "good old Svâmi"!! The man, no doubt, is very good; but from what I gather in your letter, if he teaches you anything you say to me, *i.e.*, anything save an impersonal, *non*-thinking and *non*-intelligent Principle they call Parabrahm, then he will not be teaching you the *true spirit* of that philosophy, not from its esoteric aspect, at any rate. However, this is no business of mine. You are, of course, at liberty to try and learn *something*, since it seems that we could teach you *nothing*.

Only since two professors of two different schools—like the two proverbial cooks in the matter of sauce—can succeed but in making confusion still worse confounded, I believe I had better retire from the field of competition altogether; at any rate, until you think yourself in a better position to understand and appreciate our teachings, as you kindly express it.

We are held and described by some persons as no better than refined or "cultured tântrikas"? Well, we ought to feel grateful for the prefixed adjective, since it would have been as easy for our would-be biographers to call us *unrefined* tântrikas. Moreover, the easy way with which you notify us of the comparison made, makes me feel confident of the fact that you know little, if anything, about the professors of that sect; otherwise, you would have hardly, as a gentleman, given room to such a simile in your letters. One more word will suffice. The "tântrikas"—at least the modern sect, for over 400 years—observe rites and ceremonies, the fitting description of which will never be attempted by the pen of one of our Brotherhood.

In the light of the Europeans, "character" for adepts and ascetics seems as indispensable as to servant-maids. We are sorry we are unable to satisfy, at present, the curiosity of our well-wishers as to our real worth.

I cannot leave unnoticed the remark that your want of progress has been due to the fact that you were not allowed to come to us and be taught personally. No more than yourself was Mr. Sinnett accorded any such privilege. Yet he seems to understand perfectly well whatever he is taught, and even the few hazy points upon subjects of an extremely abstruse nature will be very soon cleared for him. Nor have we ever had "one word of unpleasantness" between us—not even between him and M., whose bluntness in speaking out his mind is often very great,[43] and, since you bring out again the question of our supposed identity with the "O.G." . . . the question in days of yore, I will, with your permission, have a few words to say to this. Even now, you confess that you are *not* sure, that you cannot tell whether I am not D. or a "Spirit of the high Eastern plane" (the latter being an honour, indeed, after being suspected as a tântrika); *ergo, you* think, I "cannot honestly wonder" at your doubts. No; I wonder at nothing, for I knew all this long ago. *Some day* this and much more will be demonstrated by you objectively—*subjective* proof being no proof at all. I have been more than once suspected by you of taking my knowledge and impressions about you and other persons and things in the outside world from Olcott's and the O. L.'s[44] heads. Kindly give thought to the following law, when alluding to my taking my ideas of you "out of the Old Lady's head or Olcott's, or any one else's". It is a familiar saying that a well-matched couple "grow together," so as to come to a close resemblance in features as well as in mind. But do you know that between adept and chela—Máster and Pupil—there gradually forms a closer tie; for the psychic interchange is regulated scientifically; whereas between husband and wife unaided nature is left to herself. As the water in a full tank runs into an empty one which it is connected with; and as the common level will be sooner or later reached according to the capacity of the feed-pipe, so does the knowledge of the adept flow to the chela; and the chela attains the adept-level according to his receptive capacities. At the same time the chela, being an individual, a separate evolution, unconsciously imparts to the Master the quality of his accumulated mentality. The Master absorbs *his* knowledge, and, if it is a question of language he does not know, the Master will get the chela's linguistic accumulations just as they are—idioms and all—unless he takes the trouble to sift and remodel the phrases when using. Proof—M .·. who does not know English [45] and has to use Olcott's or the O.L.'s language. So you see it is quite possible for *me* to catch H.P.B.'s or any other chela's ideas about you without meaning to do you any injustice; for whenever we find such ideas—unless trifling—we never proceed to judge and render our sentences merely on the testimony of such borrowed light; but always ascertain independently and for ourselves whether the ideas so reflected in us are right or wrong.

And now a few words about your letter of the 5th ultimo. However great the services—in connection with literary worth—rendered us by

Mr. . . ., the President of the . . . has nevertheless, done nothing whatever for his Branch. You have dropped it out of your thoughts—to all intents and purposes, my dear brother, from the first. All your energies were devoted to the comprehension of our philosophy, and the knowledge and acquirements of our secret doctrines. You have done a good deal in this direction and I thank you heartily. Yet no attempt was ever made to organize your Branch on a firm foundation, not even regular meetings held; on the plea that you were not allowed to know *all*, you gave your fellows *nothing*. And since you say you appreciate sincerity, then I will say more. Many of the fellows of the . . . Branch who complained that out of the only two Englishmen—men of real education and learning—who took an active part in the work of the Society, the President of the . . ., while leaving many a letter unanswered from fellows loyal and devoted to the cause, and paying little, if any, attention to his own Branch, was known to hold a most friendly correspondence with one who was publicly and widely known as the greatest enemy of the Founders, their traducer and slanderer and the open opponent of the Society. I speak, as you already know, of . . . a man who has done more to injure the Society and the cause than all the . . . papers put together. In one of your latest letters you do me the honour to say that you firmly believe me a "gentleman," incapable of an ungentlemanly act. Last year, during a Council Meeting in your billiard room, and in the presence of several Theosophists, when through H.P.B., I advised you to offer . . . to resign, since he entertained such a miserable opinion of the Founders—you felt very indignant at the suggestion and declared publicly that I was "*no* gentleman". This little contradiction and *change* of opinion must not prevent me from telling you again, that had . . . then and there been shown the necessity of resigning under rules 16 and 17, the cause would not have suffered as it has, and he himself would not have appeared in the contemptible light of (*a*) a *traitor* who forfeits his *word of honour* as a Theosophist; (*b*) an untruthful man, deliberately telling falsehoods; and (*c*) when he had finally left the Society, a reviler of innocent persons.

The harm he has done, and the falsehoods he told are detailed in . . . letter to me which I send you. The fact alone that he accused H.P.B., who had seen him but once in her life, and long after he had joined, of confessing to him that the Society had a *political* object, and that she had asked him to make a political programme for her, shows you the man as a liar. If he has a letter to that effect from H.P.B., why does he not produce it? You may, if you like, regard me once more as *no* gentleman, but when I read the letter he wrote to you in which he speaks of the disintegration of the . . . Society and makes other false suggestions, I wondered from the bottom of my heart that a man of your ability and discrimination, who undertakes to fathom that which no *uninitiate* has ever fathomed, should be so taken in by an ambitious and vain little man who succeeded in striking the right chord in your heart and plays upon it ever since! Yes; he was once upon a time an honest, sincere man; he has some good qualities in him, that may be called redeeming qualities; with all that, he has shown that to achieve an object and gain an advantage over those he hates more than the Founders, if possible, he could also lie and resort to dishonourable actions. But enough of him—who is mentioned here simply in connection with your resignation as President of the . . . For, when the Chohan and M., after calling repeatedly my attention to the fact that great harm was done to the cause by . . . vilifications (and by his boasting that he was supported by the . . . of the . . . himself, *whom he forced to quit* that Society of humbugs and myths), told me that it was nigh time that something should be done to stop such a state of things, I had but to confess that they were right and I wrong. It was I, certainly, who suggested to . . . the advisability of such a change; and I am glad you liked the idea. You prefer, as you tell me, to be "simply a zealous though independent theosophist, a simple member of the Society, with whose objects—however faulty the system . . . you sympathize from the bottom of your heart," and Mr. Sinnett—who had no more, and perhaps less, objective certainty of our identity than you had—is nevertheless perfectly willing to work with us without ever feeling his loyalty wavering or his inability to defend "the system and policy of our order". Thus, every one feels himself in his right place. Of course, no honest man could associate with us once he felt a "conviction" that our system was "quite wrong"; and one, moreover, who believes, as you do, that since we broach some theories to which you cannot subscribe, you should not trouble yourself even about that portion of our philosophy which is true. Had I any intention of arguing, I might perhaps remark that the latter is a most easy method of burking all the sciences as well as all religious systems; for there is not one in which false facts and unproven and even the *wildest* theories do not abound. But I prefer to drop the question. To close, I may frankly confess that I rejoice to find you believing that "as an independent member of the Society I (you) shall probably be more useful and more able to do good" than you have hitherto been. I rejoice, but I *cannot help knowing* that many a change will yet occur in you before you find yourself finally settled in your ideas. Pardon me, dear Brother; I would not give you pain, but such is *my* opinion—and I abide by it.

You ask me to get the "O. L." to refrain from proposing you for the council. I do not believe there is the slightest danger of her doing it. I know, in fact, that she is the last person in the world to propose you *now*. Rightly or wrongly she feels herself injured by you to the very root of her heart; and, I am bound to confess, that—no doubt unwillingly—yet you *have* hurt her feelings very deeply upon several occasions.

Nevertheless, permit me to sign myself your obedient servant. Whenever you need me, and when you have done your study with the "Svâmi"—then I will be again at your service.

Yours faithfully,

K. H.

LETTER XXXI [46]

Question:—People of Guzerat are simple; they have a religious turn of mind, but they have been entangled in sectarian religions.

This is not peculiar to Guzerat. Almost everywhere it is so.—K. H.

Question :—Can I bring them from exoteric religion to esoteric ?

Not the work of a day nor of a few years. India has been going down for thousands of years. She must take equally long for her regeneration. The duty of the philanthropist is to work with the tide and assist the onward impulse.—K. H.

Question :—I wish to form a club . . . to discuss . . . "Sanatana Dharma"; can I succeed ?

No effort is ever lost. Every cause must produce its effects. The result may vary according to the circumstances which form a part of the cause. It is always wiser to work and force the current of events than to wait for time—a habit which has demoralised the Hindus and degenerated the country.—K. H.

Question :—If people can see phenomena they will listen . . . should I get the assistance of a high chela . . . in time of absolute necessity ?

Those who are carried away by phenomena are generally the ones who being under the dominion of Mâyâ are thus unable and incompetent to study or understand the philosophy. Exhibition of phenomena in such cases is not only a waste of power, but positively injurious. In some it encourages superstition, while in others it develops the latent germ of hostility towards philanthropists who would resort to such phenomena being shown. Both the extremes are prejudicial to real human progress, which is happiness. For a time, wonders may attract a mob, but that is no step towards the regeneration of humanity. As Subba Row[47] has explained to you, the aim of the philanthropist should be the spiritual enlightenment of his fellowmen. And whoever works unselfishly to that goal necessarily puts himself in magnetic communication with our chelas and ourselves. Subba Row is the best person to advise you, but he is not a very good correspondent. Whatever has to be learnt from him must be done verbally.

K. H.

LETTER XXXII [48]

SPHERES of influence can be found everywhere. The first object of the T.S. is philanthropy. The true Theosophist is a philanthropist—" not for himself but for the world he lives!" This, and philosophy, the right comprehension of life and its mysteries, will give the "necessary basis" and show the right path to pursue. Yet the best "sphere of influence" for the applicant is now in [his own land].

K. H.

LETTER XXXIII [49]

MY reference to "philanthropy" was meant in its broadest sense, and to draw attention to the absolute need of the "doctrine of the heart" as opposed to that which is merely "of the eye". And before, I have written that our Society is not a mere intellectual school for occultism, and those greater than we have said [50] that he who thinks the task of working for others too hard had better not undertake it. The moral and spiritual sufferings of the world are more important and need help and cure more than science needs aid from us in any field of discovery. "He that hath ears to hear, let him hear."

K. H.

MARGINAL LETTERS

LETTER XXXIV [51]

77 Elgin Crescent

Notting Hill

Sept. 8th [1882]

Dear Madam,

I hereby forward my subscription for *The Theosophist* for next year. I need hardly tell you how much I value your paper from which I am continually learning something.

As members (myself and mother) of the B. T. S. [52] I take this opportunity of saying that I trust the private religious opinions of individuals will not lead to a separation from the parent society, as I cannot conceive but that by so doing we should be taking a retrograde step away from any chance of obtaining further enlightenment.

We have of course read Colonel Olcott's letter addressed to the members of the B.T.S. and agree with the views it expresses.

Please accept
dear Madam
our sincere good wishes for your success in your arduous labours.

Yours sincerely,

Francesca Arundale

A GOOD, *EARNEST* THEOSOPHIST, A MYSTIC WHOSE CO-OPERATION OUGHT TO BE SECURED THRO' YOU.

K. H.

LETTER XXXV [53]

YOU better come. Give *my thanks* to your father. He has done what he could, and—could do no more.

K. H.

LETTER XXXVI [54]

THE days of his blindness will return again, he will turn once more away from truth's bright face.

M.

LETTER XXXVII [55]

TAKE courage. I am pleased with you. Keep your own counsel, and believe in your better intuitions. The little man has *failed* and will reap his reward. Silence meanwhile.

K. H.

THE FRENCH LETTER OF 1870

LETTER XXXVIII [56]

A l'Honorable,

Très Honorable Dame,

Nadyéjda Andréewna Fadeew,

Odessa.

Les nobles parents de Mad. H. Blavatsky n'ont aucune cause de se désoler. Leur fille et nièce n'a point quitté ce monde. Elle vit et désire faire savoir à ceux qu'elle aime, qu'elle se porte bien et se sent fort heureuse dans la retraite lointaine et inconnue qu'elle s'est choisie. Elle a été bien malade, mais, ne l'est plus : car grâce à la protection du Seigneur Sangyas elle a trouvé des amis devoués qui en prennent soin physiquement et spirituellement. Que les dames de sa maison se tranquillisent donc. Avant que 18 lunes nouvelles se lèvent—elle sera revenue dans sa famille.

TRANSLATION

To the Honourable,

Most Honourable Lady,

Nadyejda Andreewna Fadeew,

Odessa.

The noble relations of Mad. H. Blavatsky have no cause whatsoever for grief. Their daughter and niece has not left this world at all. She is living, and desires to make known to those whom she loves that she is well and quite happy in the distant and unknown retreat which she has selected for herself. She has been very ill, but is so no longer ; for under the protection of the Lord Sangyas [Buddha] she has found devoted friends who guard her physically and spiritually. The ladies of her house should therefore remain tranquil. Before 18 new moons shall have risen, she will return to her family.

ON THE USE OF THE LETTERS BY THEOSOPHICAL WRITERS

LETTER XXXIX [57]

YOU may, if you choose so, or find necessity for it, use in "Man" [58] or in any other book you may chance to be collaborating for, anything I may have said in relation to our secret doctrines in any of my letters to Messrs. Hume or Sinnett. Those portions that were private have never been allowed by them to be copied by anyone; and those which are so copied have by the very fact become theosophical property. Besides, copies of my letters—at any rate those that contained my *teachings*—have always been sent by my order to Damodar and Upasika, and some of the portions even used in *The Theosophist*. You are at liberty to even copy them *verbatim* and without quotation marks—I will not call it "plagiarism" . . . From the right point of view, if you will know, it is only the expression of another person's *original* ideas, some independent sentence, a thought, which in its brief completeness is capable of being constructed into a wise motto or maxim, that could be constituted into what is regarded as *plagiarism*—the pilfering of another person's "brain property". There is not a book but is the shadow of some other book, the concrete image, very often, of the *astral body* of it in some other work upon the same or approximate subject. I agree entirely with Dr. Cromwell when he says that " true talent will become original in the very act of engaging itself with the ideas of others"; nay, will often *convert the dross* of previous authors into the golden ore that shines forth to the world as its own peculiar creation. " From a series of extravagant and weak Italian romances, Shakespeare took the plots, the characters, and the major part of the incidents of those dramatic works which have exalted his name, as an *original* writer, above that of every other in the annals of literature."

Thus not only you, a chela of mine, but anyone else is at liberty to take anything, whole pages, if thought proper, from any of my "copied" letters and convert their "dross" into pure ore of gold, provided they have well grasped the thought. Show this to . . . who was already told the same.

K. H.

THE FUTURE OF THE T.S.

LETTER XL [59]

YOU have still to learn that so long as there are three men worthy of our Lord's blessing [60] in the T.S., it can never be destroyed.

M.

NOTES

1. Letter I, p. 3

This is the only letter from the Maha-Chohan, the great Adept "to whose insight the future lies like an open page". (See Letter XVI.) Written in 1881. Transcribed from a copy with C. W. Leadbeater. Parts of this letter were quoted by H. P. B. in *Lucifer*, Vol. II. August 1888, pp. 432-3.

2. Letter II, p. 13

Received at Adyar on December 26th, 1883, and opened in the presence, among others, of Dr. (Sir) S. Subramania Iyer, as described in *The Theosophist*, Vol. V. *Supplement* No. 2 of February, 1884, p. 31. Transcribed from a copy in the possession of Pandit Pran Nath of Gwalior.

3. Letter III, p. 14

Received in London in 1884. Transcribed direct from the original at Adyar.

4. Letter III, p. 19

Parent Society.

5. Letter IV, p. 20

Received in 1884 at Elberfeld, Germany. Addressed to Miss Francesca Arundale, Treasurer of the London Lodge. Transcribed from a copy in the handwriting of C. W. Leadbeater. Published in *The Theosophist*, Oct. 1917, in the article "Some Reminiscences of a Veteran Theosophist," by Francesca Arundale.

6. Letter IV, p. 22

The then recently formed Branch of the T. S. at Elberfeld.

7. Letter V, p. 25

This is one of the most striking documents now at Adyar. It consists of a Pledge to the Masters, written out by Miss Arundale, and signed by all those who made up the "Inner Group" of the London Lodge. But both the Masters M. and K. H., and also H. P. B., have written on the document. The part in the handwriting of Miss Arundale is printed in small letters; that in the handwriting of H. P. B. in large letters; and that in the handwriting of the Masters, in large capitals. It will be noted that in the second paragraph the Master K. H. has added a phrase in parenthesis, as also after the addition by H. P. B. At the end of the Pledge in the handwriting of Miss Arundale, and before there begin the signatures of the members of the Group, there are in the document four vacant lines; in these vacant lines the message of the two Masters is written; hence the words "the undersigned" refers to the signatories of the Group whose names come below the handwriting of the Masters. Written across the statement of the Master K. H. there appears the one word "Approved" in the handwriting of the Master M., followed by his initial.

8. Letter VI, p. 31

Received by Pandit Pran Nath of Gwalior in January, 1884. Transcribed direct from the original. The Letter of the Master is in reply to the following:

ALLAHABAD

10-1-84

MOST REVD. MASTER K. H.,

Do I tread the right path? Is my present way of life conducive to spiritual advancement? Am I capable of greatly influencing my next birth by good karmas in this life by strenuously following the bent of my heart as it is at present? What should I do to have the honour of prostrating myself at your blessed feet?

I am,

Yours most respectfully,

PRAN NATH, F.T.S.

9. Letter VII, p. 32

Transcribed direct from the original at Adyar. This and the following letter were received by C. W. Leadbeater, the former on the morning of the 31st October, 1884, and the latter at midnight of the same day. The first letter was received by post, and bears the London postmark, "Kensington, Oct. 30—84"; the second letter was "precipitated" in the presence of C. W. L.

10. Letter VII, p. 32

At this time C. W. L. was closely investigating Spiritualism, and was attending many of the séances of William Eglinton, one of whose spirit-guides was named "Ernest". Ernest assured C. W. L. that he knew of the existence of the Masters, and intimated his readiness to deliver a letter to the Master K. H. The letter was written, and put by Mr. Eglinton in the box kept for communications for the spirit-guides. C.W.L. was notified by Mr. Eglinton after a few days that the letter had disappeared from the box. At subsequent séances, when enquiry was made from Ernest as to what happened to the letter, Ernest assured C. W. L. that it had been duly delivered.

11. Letter VII, p. 32

Upasika is a name often used for H. P. B. in the Letters ; the word is from Buddhism, where it denotes a Lay Disciple, or one who has taken special vows, but is not technically a monk or nun.

12. Letter VII, p. 33

C. W. L. at the time of receiving this letter was an officiating priest of the Church of England ; it was at this time that an attempt was made by the Christian missionaries at Madras to wreck the Theosophical Society in what is known as the " Coulomb affair ".

13. Letter VII, p. 35

" Our Lord's the Tathāgata's memory." This is a most striking phrase, understood only many long years after the receipt of the letter. It refers to incidents of past lives of long ago, when C. W. L. had seen the Great Lord face to face. It is as if the Master tried in this manner to go behind the personality of C. W. L. direct to the Ego, in whose consciousness the great truths existed as matters of direct knowledge.

14. Letter VIII, p. 35

Transcribed direct from the original at Adyar. On receipt of Letter VII, C.W.L., who was living at Liphook, Hampshire, came up at once to London to see H.P.B., and intimated to her his determination to go at once to Adyar. At midnight of that day this letter was received.

15. Letter IX, p. 36

Reprinted from *The Link*, November, 1908. The date, from the context, is evidently the end of 1883.

16. Letter IX, p. 37

This "P.S." occurs as the first part of Letter VI, and so it would seem that the Master used here as a postscript what he had said in answer to the question of Pandit Pran Nath.

17. Letter X, p. 37

Transcribed direct from the original at Adyar.

18. Letter XI, p. 38

Transcribed direct from the original at Adyar.

19. Letter XII, p. 41

This Letter is found in "Echoes from the Past," *The Theosophist*, December, 1907, p. 259, where it is reprinted from the *Indian Mirror* of Calcutta, of April 14, 1882.

20. Letter XIII, p. 42

This letter refers to H.P.B. Transcribed direct from the original at Adyar.

21. Letter XIV, p. 42

Transcribed direct from the original at Adyar. Mr. Sinnett at this time was the editor of the powerful English anti-Indian newspaper, the *Pioneer* of Allahabad. On Mr. Sinnett's accepting Theosophy, the tone of the paper underwent a change which was not to the taste of the proprietors of the paper. The Master K. H. desired that a newspaper, to be called *The Phoenix*, should be started with Indian capital, but with Mr. Sinnett as editor. The capital necessary, however, was not subscribed.

22. Letter XIV, p. 43

Norendro Nath Sen, the founder and editor of the *Indian Mirror* of Calcutta.

23. Letter XV, p. 43

Transcribed direct from the original at Adyar, The only letter which I have so far seen where the Master signs his full name, making thereby his warning of especial significance. The recipient finally did so doubt, and "drop out".

24. Letter XVI, p. 47

Transcribed direct from the original at Adyar. To it is attached a card in the handwriting of Colonel Olcott as follows: "Letter to H. S. O. *formed in his own hand* by Master K. H. during a night visit to him, in his Camp at the Maidan, outside Lahore." (See *O. D. L.*)

Colonel Olcott in *Old Diary Leaves*, Third Series, pp. 36-7, describes the incident of receiving this letter.

25. Letter XVI, p. 47

Refers to the visit of the Master M. to Colonel Olcott in New York, described in *Old Diary Leaves*, First Series, pp. 379, 380. The "objective proof" is the *fehta* or turban, now at Adyar, which the Master M. left with the Colonel as a proof that his visit was not a "Maya" but was a reality.

26. Letter XVI, p. 47

See *Old Diary Leaves*, Third Series, p. 37.

27. Letter XVII, p. 48

Transcribed direct from the original at Adyar, which has the following attached to it on a card in the handwriting of Colonel Olcott: "Note to H. S. O. from Master K, H. to prepare him for a visit in the physical body, in his tent at Lahore." (See *O. D. L.*) This second visit is described by Colonel Olcott in *Old Diary Leaves*. Third Series, p. 42, and by Mr. W. T. Brown, who was present with him, in his pamphlet, *Some Experiences in India*. The Messenger referred to is the Master D. K.

28. Letter XVIII, p. 48

Reprinted from *The Theosophist*, Feb. 1908, with the following explanatory note by Colonel Olcott: "Dropped in railway carriage, April 5th, 1884, as I was reading a lot of letters from L.L., the particulars about the Kingsford-Sinnett quarrel. This letter fell just as I was noting a paragraph in B.K.'s letter about the Mahatmas. Present in the railway carriage only Mohini and myself. H.S.O." See also *Old Diary Leaves*, Third Series, pp. 90, 91.

29. Letter XIX, p. 50

There is little doubt, not only from the context, but also from one fact mentioned by Colonel Olcott, that this letter was received in August 1888. But, curiously, it seems from reading *Old Diary Leaves*, Third Series, p. 91, as if it were received in 1883. Colonel Olcott there quotes from this Letter, and connects it with the difficulties of 1884 in the London Lodge, concerning which instructions were given to him in Letter XVIII. Colonel Olcott mentions that Letter XIX was "received phenomenally in my cabin on board the 'Shannon,' the day before we reached Brindisi" (p. 91). But he sailed from Bombay for London on P. & O. Mail Steamer *Shannon* on August 7th, 1888, as reported in *The Theosophist*, *Supplement*, September 1888, p. ciii. Furthermore, in the body of the Letter itself the Master says: "since 1885 I have not written"; and C. W. L., who is mentioned at the end of the letter, did not come out to India till the end of 1884. It would seem, therefore, that Colonel Olcott, in narrating events about the London Lodge, took this letter about the "situation" in 1888 to refer to the situation in 1884.

It is perhaps worth mentioning the urgency of the situation in 1888. The T. S. was founded in 1875, and for the first seven years of its life it was being tested in several different ways. In one respect it failed, and this was because of its disinclination to accept openly the direct guidance of the Society by the "Brothers," *i.e.*, the Masters, who formed the "First Section" of the Society. By 1882 the majority of members in the T.S. accepted the occult philosophy given by the Masters, but refused to accept the occult guidance given by the Masters through their Chelas in the outer administration of the Society. At the end of the first cycle, in 1882, the Masters, therefore, retired somewhat into the background, so far as the Society's outer affairs were concerned, and gave their directions only to a few selected individuals.

When the second cycle was nearing completion, in 1889, H.P.B. was anxious to make another effort to strengthen the occult links between the T.S. and the Masters. She was successful in her effort, and the *E.S.T.* was the result. But before the *E.S.T.* could be organised, many difficulties arose, and it was as a result of this Letter XIX received by Colonel Olcott that he smoothed matters in the Society's administration, so that the *E.S.T.* might do its work under the sole direction of H.P.B., without interfering in, or being interfered with, by the democratic organisation of the T.S. It was not, however, till 1907 that the T.S. fully regained its original position, with the Masters of the Wisdom as once more the "First Section" of the Society.

30. Letter XIX, p. 55

I do not know which Adept is referred to by this symbol, nor have I been able to find out what was the incident at Adyar to which the Master refers.

31. Letter XX, p. 56

Transcribed direct from the original at Adyar.

32. Letter XXI, p. 63

This Letter appears in the pamphlet *Some Experiences in India*, by W. T. Brown, B.L., F.T.S., a member of the London Lodge of the T.S., who came out to India in 1883. He was present with Colonel Olcott at Lahore, when the incident took place referred to in Letters XVI and XVII. At this time the Master K. H. had come to India from Tibet, and Mr. Brown saw him, as narrated in the pamphlet mentioned above.

33. Letter XXI, p. 63

The Master K. H. is by birth a Kashmiri Brahman. Mr. Brown was at this time with Colonel Olcott at Jammu, Kashmir, as guest of the then Maharaja of Kashmir; the letter was received "enclosed in an envelope, which had been addressed by Madame G—, but had come by post from Germany. This was very significant, because it proved, to my mind, that the Master was aware of the part which Madame G—had had in bringing me into the light of Theosophy." The lady referred to is probably Madame Gebhard. Mr. W. T. Brown—"Poor

Brown"—later left the T.S. See *Old Diary Leaves*, Third Series, Chapters III and XXIII.

34. Letter XXII, p. 63

Received by Mr. W. T. Brown on December 17th, 1883, as narrated in his pamphlet. From a copy in the possession of Pandit Pran Nath of Gwalior. Following the advice given, Mr. Brown wrote of his experiences in the pamphlet mentioned above.

35. Letter XXIII, p. 67

Transcribed direct from the original at Adyar.

36. Letter XXIV, p. 67

Transcribed direct from the original at Adyar.

37. Letter XXV, p. 70

Received at Adyar, December 1883, by Prince Harisinghji Rupsinghji of the Ruling Family of Bhavnagar. Reprinted from *The Theosophist, Supplement*, June 1884, p. 87.

38. Letter XXVI, p. 73

Transcribed direct from the original at Adyar. It is written on a slip of paper, and must have been annexed to an article sent to *The Theosophist*, which during H. P. B.'s absence was under the direction of Damodar K. Mavalankar. The article referred to appears in *The Theosophist, Supplement*, February 1884, p. 31. It is a letter by V. Coopooswamy Iyer, M.A., F.T.S., of Madura, who describes the incident of a letter which was phenomenally delivered in the presence of several people. "Subram's statement" refers to the letter of (now Dr.) S. Subramania Iyer, B.L., then High Court Vakil, Madura, who also describes certain phenomena which happened in his presence.

39. Letter XXVII, p. 73

Transcribed direct from the original at Adyar. Received by Damodar K. Mavalankar, and has marked in the corner: "Rd. 5 a.m., 27-2-84." D. K. M. left for Tibet in April 1885. See *Old Diary Leaves*, Third Series, Ch. XV, p. 318. The Letter was reprinted in *The Theosophist*, November 1908, p. 173.

40. Letter XXVIII, p. 74

Reprinted from *The Theosophist*, Feb. 1908, p. 391, where it is stated the letter was received by Dr. F. Hartmann at Adyar in 1884, when both the Founders were in Europe. "D." is evidently D.M.K.

41. Letter XXIX, p. 75

Reprinted from a copy in the possession of C.W.L.; the Letter is reprinted in *The Theosophist*, December 1907, p. 260, with a note to the effect that on the 5th June, 1886, Mr. Tookaram Tatya posted at Bombay a letter to Colonel Olcott. When the letter was delivered on June 7th at Adyar, the Letter of the Master was inscribed on a blank page. The letter refers to D. M. K. who, after many hardships and privations, crossed to Tibet and reached the Home of his Master.

42. Letter XXX, p. 79

This is evidently one of the letters to Mr. A. O. Hume, written in 1881 or 1882. Reprinted from *The Theosophist*, June 1907, pp. 702-6.

43. Letter XXX, p. 81

Refers to the Letters written by the Master M. to Mr. Sinnett and Mr. Hume. These Letters of the Master, not yet published, reveal a Personality whose style is direct and incisive, and most refreshing in its candour.

44. Letter XXX, p. 82

" O. L. " were the letters often used for H. P. B.—the " Old Lady ".

45. Letter XXX, p. 83

This was in 1882. So unessential evidently are words and phrases, compared to the *thought* of the thinker, that I have not been able to find the least trace, in the Letters of the Master M., of the personal idiosyncrasies of thought of either H. P. B. or H. S. O. A giant may use a child's toy hammer, but the power behind the blow is that of a giant's arm and not that of a child.

46. Letter XXXI, p. 89

The Questions were propounded in March 1884 by Mr. Navatamram Ootamram Trivedi of Surat. Reprinted from *The Theosophist*, July 1907, pp. 782-3.

47. Letter XXXI, p. 91

The late T. Subba Row, one of the pupils of the Master M., who collaborated with H. P. B. in the work of the earlier volumes of *The Theosophist*. His many Articles have been gathered together in the volume *A Collection of Esoteric Writings of T. Subba Row, F. T. S., B.A., B.L.*, Bombay, 1895.

48. Letter XXXII, p. 92

Reprinted from *The Theosophist*, November 1907, p. 167. This letter and the following are printed in *The Theosophist* as if making one letter ; as it seems to me that they might be from two distinct letters, I have separated them.

49. Letter XXXIII, p. 92

Reprinted from *The Theosophist*, November 1907, p. 167.

50. Letter XXXIII, p. 92

Refers to the first Letter in this collection, see p. 11.

51. Letter XXXIV, p. 97

In the communications received from the Masters, many instructions were given in comments upon letters; these directions were written upon the letters themselves, sometimes on any available blank space, and sometimes across the writing. Many such marginal Notes exist, of which this and the three following are examples. This Letter is one written by Miss F. Arundale, and the comment of the Master was written during transit in the post. Transcribed direct from the original at Adyar.

52. Letter XXXIV, p. 97

British Theosophical Society.

53. Letter XXXV, p. 98

Transcribed direct from the original at Adyar. This brief note comes in a letter sent by H. P. B. on July 17th, 1883, from Ootacamund, Nilgiri Hills, to Mr. G. Soobiah Chetty in Madras, in which she sends him an invitation to visit her in the hills. The main part of the letter refers to Mr. G. Muttuswamy Chetty, a Judge of the Small Causes Court of Madras, and father of Mr. G Soobiah Chetty. Mr. G. Muttuswamy Chetty received *in Tamil* a letter, posted at Amritsar, from the Master K.H., the translation of which, I am informed, was as follows: "Sinnett's paper is the only saviour for India. You must work towards it. Koot-hoomi." On receipt of this, Mr. Muttuswamy Chetty tried among his friends to raise something towards the capital required for *The Phoenix* newspaper. (See Letter XIV.) He was not, however, successful.

54. Letter XXXVI, p. 98

This brief but striking statement appears on the fly-leaf of a large illustrated edition of *The Light of Asia*, now at Adyar, presented to H. P. B. On the fly-leaf of the book is written: "H. P. Blavatsky from her friend, Gerard Brown Finch." Mr. Finch was President of the London Lodge, T. S., in 1884. He soon afterwards "dropped out".

55. Letter XXXVII, p. 98

Transcribed direct from the original at Adyar. This occurs written across a folded letter written by H. P. B. at Elberfeld, June 23rd, 1886, to C. W. L., then in Ceylon. The Master's message was precipitated in transit. The letter of H. P. B. to C. W. L. was about an Indian chela of the Master who was in Germany with her, but who turned against her. "The little man has failed," refers to this individual, who thus "dropped out".

56. Letter XXXVIII, p. 101

This is the earliest letter written by any of the Masters, written in 1870, five years before the T. S. was founded. The original, which is in French, exists now at Adyar. It is in the now well-known handwriting of the Master K. H. to H. P. B's aunt, Madame Nadejda Fadeeff; she wrote on June 26th, 1884, from Paris to Colonel Olcott about this Letter, and describing the anxiety of H. P. B's relations, who had no news of her for some years, says as follows:

> All our researches had ended in nothing. We were ready to believe her dead, when—I think it was about the year 1870, or possibly later—I received a letter from him whom I believe you call "K.H.," which was brought to me in the most incomprehensible and mysterious manner, by a

messenger of Asiatic appearance, *who then disappeared before my very eyes.* This letter, which begged me not to fear anything, and which announced that she was in safety —I have still at Odessa. Immediately upon my return I shall send it you, and I shall be very pleased if it can be of any use to you. (*Report of the Result of an Investigation into the Charges against Madame Blavatsky*, 1885, p. 94.)

Madame Fadeeff wrote ten days later from Odessa to Colonel Olcott enclosing the original Letter. In the lower left-hand corner of the envelope there is written in Russian, in pencil, in the handwriting of Madame Fadeeff, the following: "Received at Odessa, November 7, about Lelinka, probably from Tibet.—November 11, 1870. Nadejda F." *Lelinka* was H. P. B's pet name. The Letter of the Master is signed, not with his initials, K. H., but with a letter in some language not known to me. It would seem from certain remarks of the Master M., in one of his Letters, that he was the "Messenger of Asiatic appearance" who delivered the letter.

57. Letter XXXIX, p. 105

Transcribed direct from the original at Adyar.

58. Letter XXXIX, p. 106

The book, *Man: Fragments of Forgotten History, by Two Chelās in the Theosophical Society*, published in 1885.

59. Letter XL, p. 109

I have not been able to trace the original letter in which this occurs, but it is reprinted in *The Theosophist*, November 1907, p. 167.

60. Letter XL, p. 109

"Our Lord's blessing"—the blessing of the Lord Gautama Buddha.

Printed by J. R. Aria at the Vasanta Press, Adyar, Madras.